WHY DON'T

worms have legs?

By Jenny Vaughan

WHY DON'T
worms have legs?

ticktock
MEDIA

Copyright © ticktock Entertainment Ltd 2003

First published in Great Britain in 2003 by ticktock Entertainment Ltd.,

Unit 2, Orchard Business Centre, North Farm Road, Tunbridge Wells, Kent, TN2 3XF

We would like to thank: Lorna Cowan, Paul Hillyard at

The Natural History Museum and Elizabeth Wiggans.

ISBN 1 86007 382 4 pbk

ISBN 1 86007 388 3 hbk

Printed in China

A CIP catalogue record for this book is available from the British Library.

CONTENTS

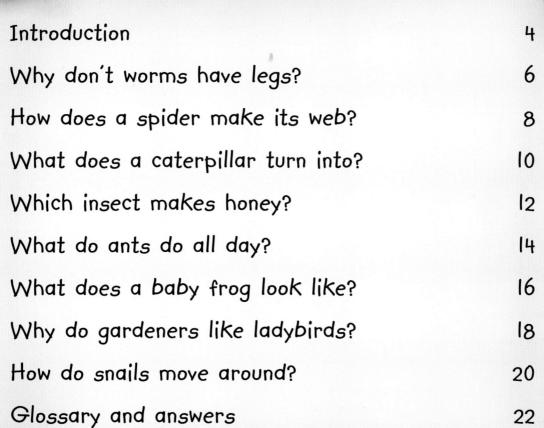

Any words appearing in the text in bold, **like this**, are explained in the Glossary.

Did you know that your garden is home to lots of little creatures?

Underground

In the water

Among the plants

Which ones have you seen? Where did you see them?

Some creatures live in water. Some live among the plants.
Some build nests, and others live underground.
But do you know what happens inside the nests?
What do they all eat? And how do they
care for their young?

Why don't worms have legs?

Worms don't have legs because they don't need them to move around under the ground.

A worm's body is made up of parts called **segments**.

There are tiny **bristles**, like hairs, on each segment.

Segments

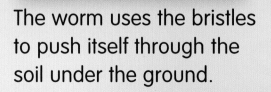

Bristles

The worm uses the bristles to push itself through the soil under the ground.

Worms eat soil, leaves and animal droppings.

Sometimes you can see the remains of the worm's meal after it has passed through the worm's body.

The remains are very good for the soil.

Do you think worms can see?

(answer on page 23)

Worms also make holes or passageways in the soil. The holes make it easier for water to reach the roots of the plants.

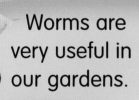

Worms are very useful in our gardens.

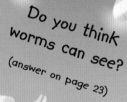

Birds like to eat them too.

Spiders live in your garden too – in webs. How does a spider make its web?

a) Using thread it makes itself

b) Using thread it gets from underground

c) Using thread it gets from plants

(You will find the answer on the next page.)

How does a spider make its web?

A spider makes its web from threads of **silk** it gets from inside its own body.

The silk is very strong, but it is very, very thin!

Different kinds of spiders make different webs. This kind is called an **orb web**.

Orb web

The spider starts with just one thread between two leaves or twigs.

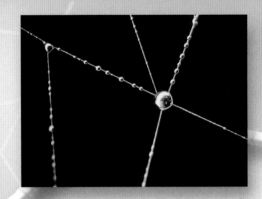

Then it makes another thread.
It fixes this to another leaf or twig.

It makes a shape like the **spokes** of a wheel.

Then it fills in the spaces between the spokes.

Which is strongest – steel wire or spider's silk?

(answer on page 23)

Trapped fly

Spiders are very useful. Their webs trap **insect pests** such as flies.

Caterpillars live on the plants in your garden. What does a caterpillar turn into?

a) A snake

b) A butterfly

c) A bigger caterpillar

What does a caterpillar turn into?

Caterpillar

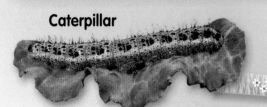

When it has grown to its full size, a caterpillar turns into a butterfly.

Caterpillars hatch from tiny eggs.

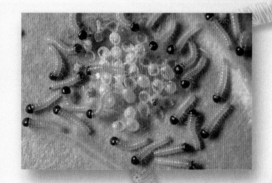

Butterfly

Each caterpillar eats and eats and grows and grows. It gets too big for its skin.

The old skin falls off. There is a new one underneath.

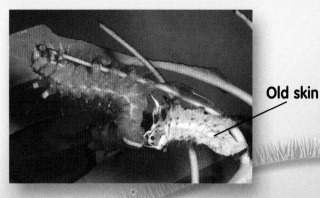

Old skin

The caterpillar goes on growing and gets another new skin. This happens several times.

After a while the caterpillar makes a shell for itself. Now it is called a **pupa**.

Pupa

What do you think happens to butterfly eggs?

(answer on page 23)

Butterfly

Something amazing happens inside the pupa. Look what comes out!

Butterflies do not eat leaves – but they do lay eggs on them.

Some insects in your garden are very busy. Which insect makes honey?

a) Butterflies make it

b) Ladybirds make it

c) Bees make it

Which insect makes honey?

Insects called bees make honey. Worker bees collect **nectar** from flowers.

They turn it into honey inside their bodies.

A bee dancing

When a bee finds flowers with plenty of nectar, it goes back to the hive and does a kind of dance.

Hive

The dance shows the other bees the direction where the flowers are. They can all collect plenty of nectar.

In the hive the bees make waxy combs that they fill with the honey.

What do you think the beekeepers do with the honey?

(answer on page 23)

Honeycomb

In the combs are the young bees. They are called **larvae**.

Larvae

Worker bees feed the larvae on honey.

Worker bee

Beekeepers collect the combs and remove the honey from them. They leave some for the bees.

Ants are everywhere in your garden. What do ants do all day?

a) They build webs
b) They look after the nest they live in
c) They eat cabbages

What do ants do all day?

Ants work hard all day looking after their nest.

Some ants are 'soldiers'. They defend the nest.

The queen ant lays eggs in the nest. Most ants are 'workers'. Some look after the eggs.

Nest entrance

Food chamber

Soldier ant

Cocoons

Worker ant

Eggs

Queen ant in chamber

Aphid

Some ants collect **honeydew** from **insects** called **aphids**.

Larvae hatch from the eggs. Workers bring food for the larvae.

Ants stroke the aphids to make them release honeydew from their bodies.

Cocoon

The larvae make **cocoons**. Inside the cocoons, they turn into adult ants. Some workers look after the cocoons.

What do you think the ants use the honeydew for?

(answer on page 23)

Rubbish is kept here

Larvae

Some creatures like frogs live in water in your garden. What does a baby frog look like?

a) A small adult frog

b) A fish

c) A young insect

What does a baby frog look like?

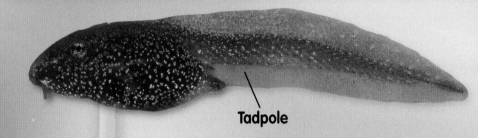

Tadpole

Baby frogs look a bit like fish. They are called tadpoles.

The tadpoles start life as tiny dots in a lump of clear jelly. This is **frogspawn.** You may find it in a pond.

Gradually, the dot changes shape and tadpoles hatch out of the frogspawn.

As the tadpoles grow bigger they change shape.

They grow legs. Their tails get smaller, then disappear.

After four months, the tadpoles have changed to frogs.

Toad

Newt

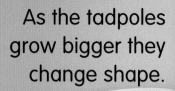

Frog

Do you think frogs can live in and out of water?

(answer on page 23)

Animals with lives like frogs are called **amphibians**. Newts, toads and salamanders are also amphibians.

Some creatures in your garden are very useful. Why do gardeners like ladybirds?

a) Because they are pretty

b) Because they eat garden pests

c) Because they eat garden weeds

Why do gardeners like ladybirds?

Ladybirds are a kind of **beetle**. Most are red with black spots.

They are helpful in the garden because they eat **insects** called **aphids**.

— Aphids

Aphids suck the juice out of plants, and the plants may die.

How many aphids do you think a ladybird can eat in one day?

(answer on page 23)

Ladybirds lay eggs. Ladybird **larvae** hatch out.

The larvae eat lots of aphids – they grow bigger and bigger. One day they will become adult ladybirds.

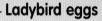
Ladybird eggs

Ladybird larvae

If there are lots of ladybirds in your garden, they will eat lots of aphids.

The plants will grow well. That's why gardeners like ladybirds.

There are many different kinds of ladybirds.

Some creatures fly, some walk and some swim. How do snails move around?

a) By using a foot
b) By burrowing under the ground
c) By rolling along the ground

How do snails move around?

A snail has a foot under its body. It moves around by using this foot to push itself along.

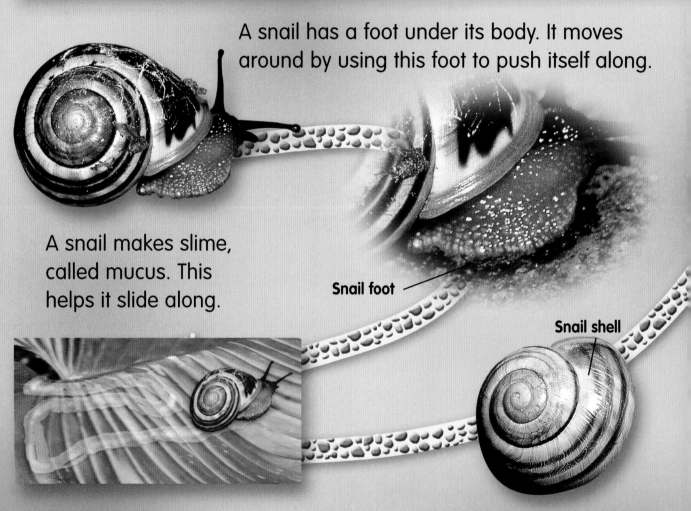

A snail makes slime, called mucus. This helps it slide along.

Snail foot

Snail shell

You can see where a snail has been because it leaves a slimy trail behind it.

The snail can hide inside its shell when it is afraid or when it is very hot outside.

Gardeners do not like snails. They eat many different kinds of plants, especially young plants.

Snails also eat vegetables and fruit.

But there are animals that eat snails.

Rats

Toad

Snakes, rats, frogs and toads all eat snails. So do some kinds of birds and **beetles**.

How fast do you think snails can travel?

(answer on page 23)

Glossary

Amphibians Animals that can live in water and on land. Frogs, toads, newts and salamanders are all different kinds of amphibians.

Aphids Small insects that suck the juices out of plants. Other names for them are greenflies (if they are green) or blackflies (if they are black).

Beetle An insect with a hard, shiny covering over its wings.

Bristles Short, stiff hairs.

Cocoons Cases made by insects from silk that comes from inside their bodies. Inside its cocoon the insect is at the stage in its life called a pupa. This is when it changes from a young insect to a grown-up one.

Frogspawn Frogs' eggs. They look like clear jelly with the young tadpole growing inside.

Toads lay the same kind of eggs.

Honeydew A liquid made in the bodies of aphids. Aphids suck the juice from plants and pass it out of their bodies as sweet honeydew.

Insects Animals that have six legs and a body in three parts. There are thousands of different kinds of insects in the world.

Larvae The young of many kinds of insects are called

larvae. One young is called a larva. Caterpillars are the larvae of butterflies.

Nectar A sweet liquid found inside flowers.

Orb web An orb web is a spider's web that is the shape of a circle.

Pests Animals that do damage to plants.

Pupa An insect that is changing from being a larva to an adult.

Segments Parts of something.

Silk Fine thread produced by spiders from inside their bodies. They use it to make webs. Some insects also make silk. The silk we use to make fabric for clothes is made by the caterpillars of a kind of moth.

Spokes The bits of a wheel that stick out from the middle to the edge.

Could you answer all the questions? Here are the answers:

Page 7: Worms have no eyes or head! But they can tell when something touches them.

Page 9: A thread of spider's silk is as strong as a piece of steel wire of the same thickness.

Page 11: Tiny caterpillars hatch from butterfly eggs.

Page 13: Beekeepers collect the honey so that we can eat it!

Page 15: Ants use honeydew to feed their larvae.

Page 17: Frogs can live in and out of water. Animals that live like this are called amphibians.

Page 18: A ladybird can eat 50 aphids in one day.

Page 21: Snails travel very slowly. It takes them about one hour to travel 20 metres.

Index

t=top, b=bottom, c=centre, l=left, r=right,
OFC=outside front cover, OBC=outside back cover

Alamy images: OFC, 9bl, 10cl, 10br, 11cr, 12tl, 12br, 13tl, 13cr, 16cl,
16cr, 16bc, 17tr, 17cr, 18bl, 19tr, 19cr, 21tl, 21tr. Ardea London: 11tc
(Pascal Goetgheluck). Corbis: 4bl, 5br, 6c, 7bl, 9tr, 15c. Ecoscene: 14tl
(Peter Currell). Science Photo Library: 6bl, 8tl, 8br, 9tc, 12tr, 15tr, 18c.